T0197555

Harry, Oh My!

Marian Kiler Hall

Illustrated By: Lyle Jakosalem

To order additional copies of this book, contact:
Xlibris
1-888-795-4274
www.Xlibris.com
Orders@Xlibris.com

Harry the Digger

Harry, the Digger, a happy dog is he,
Black and tan and white, a Basset Hound I see.
He dug a hole to find his prey;
A hunter brave, commenced to bay.

The neighbor dogs began to bark.
Harry thought it was a lark.
Came outside to save the day.
But Harry would not come away.

What if he tunneled down so deep
That it collapsed, all in a heap?
My thoughts were borderline dismay.
Would Valerie lose her dog today?

I called and whistled all in vain.
"Harry, come here!" but it was plain
Harry, the Digger, was digging still.
The flying dirt made quite a hill.

Over to Lola's I hurried to see
If she had advice she could give to me.
"Find something solid to put in the hole."
Aha! We would foil the Digger's goal!

I hunted some lumber lying around,
Six-by-six-by-two-feet to pack in the ground.
From her package of jerky, I took out a piece,
Temptation for Harry, His digging to cease.

I led him indoors and gave him his prize.
Harry, the Doggy, no longer disguised
As Harry, the Digger. I hope it will last
And all of his digging's a thing of the past.

Here is to Lola, the neighbor next door,
Whose actions were brave, and timely, but more,
Who rose to the battle, and victory bought
With lumber and jerky. What a wonderful thought!

Harry, The Model

Harry, the Doggy, a happy dog is he,
Black and tan and white, a Basset Hound I see.
Harry lay on the tile, asleep in the sun.
How peaceful he looked, after all he had done.

I brought out my paints, my brushes, and more,
Determined to have a chance to explore
The joy of painting this beautiful dog.
I sketched his position. He slept like a log.

But all of a sudden, he woke. He's away
Through his private door, and into the day,
Out under the trees, enjoying the sun,
He ran through the grass. Sleep time was done.

I thought, OK Harry, the background I'll do.
Later I'll have a chance to paint you.
Yes, Harry, the Doggy, just wanted to play.
I snatched every minute of sleep in his day.

Three days I saw a spectacular sight:
Zebra, a butterfly, danced in the light.
The painting was finished of Harry, my friend
Just one day before my vacation would end.

Harry Goodbye

I surprised Valerie. "This is for you."
And gave her the painting. "I knew"
You would have wide awake pictures of Harry to see.
This will remind you how peaceful is he

"When sleeping stretched out, in doggyland dreams,
Forgotten the troubles of dog life it seems."
What a vacation! I read through three books,
Wrote a poem, and with difficulty, painted the looks

20

Of Harry, the Doggy, within ten days stay
And visited too! What else can I say?
But the truth must be faced: my vacation is gone
I gathered my things for time rushes on.

Val seized Harry's leash, to the station we went,
I boarded the Greyhound; homeward I'm sent.
"Goodbye, Harry, the Doggy, Valerie too.
I know I shall miss you. May God bless you."

Printed in the United States
By Bookmasters